D0627095

HOW TO WIN AT
ADULTING

Your guide to living in the
GROWN UP WORLD

This third edition published in 2020
By SJG Publishing, HP22 6NF, UK

Author: Helen Redding
Illustrator: Vic McLindon
Cover design: Milestone Creative
Contents design: Seagulls

ISBN: 978-1-911517-78-8

Printed in China

10 9 8 7 6 5 4 3

CONTENTS

INTRODUCTION

You're boycotting adulthood. Perhaps you've been defined as a Millennial or Generation Y but aren't quite sure what that means. All you know is that you're terrified of being part of Generation Sensible – risk averse and far less adventurous than your parents – so you've rejected growing up. You think being a grown-up is dull, and you'd rather stick cocktail umbrellas in your eyes than acknowledge that you need to be responsible.

Yes, being an adult can be boring at times. But what's boring about being independent, self-sufficient, earning your own money, going where you want and getting on with life? They're all pretty great things to be doing. Just think of all the freedoms you get.

'Adulting' is not a hobby. You can't opt out of adulting: you are an adult whether you like it or not. It's about being responsible for yourself and functioning in the world. This book will show you how to get used to that idea and, most importantly, win at it!

What's happening
TO ME?!

**YOUR ADULTING GOAL
FOR THIS CHAPTER:**
*Give yourself a break and don't expect
miracles — you're an emerging adult.
Where's the sympathy that teenagers get?*

Remember that awkward age when you were desperate to
be a teenager and leave childhood behind? Was it frustrating,
perhaps traumatic? Well, puberty is just the start of it. There are
new challenges every step of the way as you get older, so it's no
big surprise that being expected to 'grow up' can come as an
unwelcome shock.

ARE YOU READY TO BE AN ADULT?

The laws of the land define when you're officially an adult —
generally when you can vote, drink or be tried as an adult for
a crime (now there's a cheerful thought). But life often defies
definition, making being an 'adult' a tricky concept to get your
head around. Not helpful if you're being told to grow up! So, do
you fit the bill? Can you:

- Make independent decisions?

- Accept responsibility?

■ Be financially independent?

Scary stuff, isn't it? No wonder we all head for the hills when the adulting bus calls in our town.

BECOMING AN ADULT: THE PSYCHOLOGY BIT

Before you panic, remember that you don't suddenly become an adult overnight. You're not playing with your toy cars one day, and the next deciding which SUV has the most practical trunk space. According to psychologist Jeffrey Jensen Arnett, we go through a period called 'emerging adulthood', a tumultuous time through your 20s where you're not quite – but almost – independent. It's hard to know how you should be acting, and perhaps you don't have the means to do as adults do. Can you see the parallels with puberty? And who'd want to go through that again?!

FROM CATERPILLAR TO BUTTERFLY

Professor Arnett identified five features of 'emerging adulthood':

1. **Age of identity exploration**. Who are you? What do you want out of life?

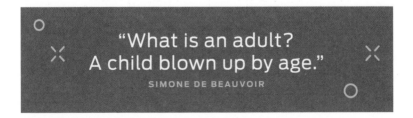

"What is an adult?
A child blown up by age."
SIMONE DE BEAUVOIR

2. **Age of instability.** The post-high school years are marked by frequent changes of home – moves to college, moving in with friends or a partner.

3. **Age of self-focus**. Freedom of choice about what you do, not limited by parents, school, or marriage and careers (yet).

4. **Age of feeling in between**. Taking responsibility for yourself but not feeling like an adult.

5. **Age of possibilities**. That wonderful feeling of optimism you have for doing bigger and better than your parents!

Sound familiar? It's up to you to embrace this and make adulting something beneficial rather than terrifying.

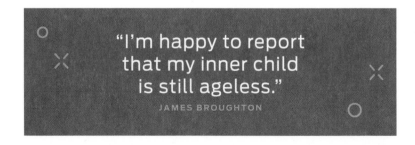

"I'm happy to report that my inner child is still ageless."

JAMES BROUGHTON

GENERATION Y,
or the Millennial

YOUR ADULTING GOAL FOR THIS CHAPTER:

Millennials get the rough end of the stick – in reality, you're not so different to any other generation being frowned upon by the one that went before. You're not going to stand by and be slated, are you?

People like to put other people in a box and stick a label on them. The problem is that stereotypes then emerge that aren't always fair or justified. So, if you're in your 20s or 30s, what are people saying about you?

THE NEW GENERATION OF ADULTS

If you were born during the 1980s or 1990s, you're considered part of Generation Y, also known as a Millennial. If that means nothing to you, don't worry: you've just been unwittingly lumped in with the millions of other people born from the loins of the Baby Boomers (Generation X). According to those in the know, you're:

- technologically savvy
- less brand loyal and not easily swayed by marketing (you've seen it all before)
- selfie-obsessed
- pampered by your parents and have a subsequent sense of self-entitlement

- a politically apathetic narcissist
- living in a perpetual state of adolescence
- incapable of commitment

Wow. You wouldn't want to include all of those on your resumé.

IN DEFENSE OF THE MILLENNIAL

Let's face it, you're a much-maligned demographic. But in your defense, it's not all roses for you. You've got an uncertain job market to contend with. You're the first generation less likely to be better off than your parents. You'll find it hard to get on the property ladder, get married and have children due to financial restraints.

All these factors make it really difficult to do those things that we associate with being an 'adult'. If you can't afford to move out of your parents' house, for example, no wonder you're struggling to forge your way into adulthood.

FELLOW MILLENNIALS

Mark Zuckerberg, Beyoncé, Mike Krieger and Kevin Systrom (creators of Instagram), Brian Chesky (co-founder of Airbnb), Prince William, Roger Federer, Serena Williams, Sean Rad (co-founder of Tinder), Jennifer Lawrence. Not such a bad bunch really.

> "Not all Millennials think alike. A demographic is not a psychographic."
>
> ANDY DUNN

A very short history

OF ADULTING

adulting/ˈadʌltɪŋ [noun]: The practice of behaving in a way characteristic of a responsible adult, especially the accomplishment of mundane but necessary tasks.

TOP 10 ADULTING TASKS

1. Get and keep a job.

2. Support yourself financially (and pay your taxes and bills).

3. Cook so that you can eat (healthily if possible – if not, just make it edible, not frozen and capable of being cooked without a microwave).

4. Maintain a to-do list and aim to tick things off it – because your mother doesn't do everything for you anymore.

5. Have goals and aspirations – but if one is still your childhood dream of being an astronaut, you might want to downgrade it a touch.

6. Look after your own health and well-being (and that includes making your own dentist and doctor appointments).

7. Do your own laundry, plus extra points for separating your whites and colors and for checking washing labels. Triple extra points for ironing. Tip: never buy 'handwash only' garments for they will just fester in the bottom of your laundry basket.

8. Live by yourself or with someone who isn't a parent, friend or stranger (who saw your ad for a lodger on Facebook).

9. Buy a house and keep it in a reasonable state because you want to, not because you have to.

10. Take responsibility for your own actions. There's no one to blame but you.

REALLY? WHEN DID LIFE GET SO BORING?

... when you started being old enough to be responsible for your own actions and their impact on others. And it's been the same through the centuries. Adulting isn't there to ruin your life. If anything, it's there to make it better, to give you freedom. But you need to embrace it like a grown-up to discover the opportunities for fun that it opens up.

> "Adults are just obsolete children ..."
>
> DR SEUSS

Mastering the art of
DECISION-MAKING

YOUR ADULTING GOAL FOR THIS CHAPTER:

To get to grips with the decision-making process, aiming to make good decisions, but understanding that things don't always go to plan – and dealing with that.

Decision-making is an unavoidable, and sometimes terrifying, part of life. As an adult, decisions are tricky as you have more choices and every one of those can have a big impact on your life. That said, no one expects you to make the right decision all the time. If you did, you just wouldn't learn anything. So, how do you approach the decision-making process when there's no one to do it for you? And we're not talking about choosing which pants to wear.

WHAT MAKES A 'GOOD' DECISION?

Should you jump the red light? No. Should you insure your car? Yes. These are easy decisions to make and you don't need to spend time thinking about them. But what if it's more complicated? Life will present you with many forks in the road. Perhaps you're thinking about changing your job or ending a relationship. These aren't decisions you jump into without thought as they have long-lasting implications. A 'good' decision is an informed decision: 'right' according to the time and context in which you make it. Right for you is very different to what is right for other people.

PRACTICAL DECISION-MAKING

Faced with an important decision, brains tend to go a bit fuzzy. If you don't find it easy to make decisions, here are some practical tips to help:

- Clearly define the decision you need to make. Keep it simple.

- Identify all your possible paths of action. Use your imagination!

- What information do you need to make the decision? Perhaps you need to research the costs. Would doing something one way rather than another affect your chances of achieving a future goal?

- Organize your thoughts. Getting your ideas down on paper is a great way to stop them swirling around inside your head and give you some clarity. Make a good, old-fashioned list of pros and cons.

- Follow your intuition. You can gather facts and make lists but there is much to be said for gut feeling. If a decision doesn't feel right, there's a pretty good chance it isn't.

> "Make a decision and watch your life move forward."
> OPRAH WINFREY

GOING TO BED EARLY, NOT GOING OUT, NO CAKE;

– – – –

MY MOM'S PUNISHMENTS ARE NOW MY ADULTING GOALS.

- Don't rely on other people. All well and good to take on board advice from other people, but remember that it's you, not them, who needs to live with the decision.

- Forget your fear. What decision would you make it you weren't fearful of the outcome? Set aside your worries and you'll find your options broaden.

- Keep your conscience clean. Don't be pressured into something you feel uncomfortable with. If a course of action would achieve your goal but leave you feeling guilty for the next 20 years, step away from that option!

- Have a cooling down period. When you've made your decision, give yourself some time to let it sink in before you act on it. Sleep on it and if your stomach turns when you wake up, perhaps you need to rethink.

- You've made the decision – what next? Think about what you need to do to implement your decision. But be flexible.

Life's a wobbly path, so don't be downhearted if reaching your goal takes you down some twists and turns.

DON'T BE OVERWHELMED

No one said that making decisions is easy. Decisions precede change, and it's absolutely normal to feel nervous about change – even paralyzed by it – whatever your age and experience. If you follow the practical tips above, hopefully you can minimize the painfulness of the process. Remember, you don't have to make a decision that makes you unhappy. One of the joys of being an adult is that you have more choices available to you – so don't forget that next time you bemoan being a grown-up!

HELP! I'VE MADE A REALLY BAD DECISION!

DON'T PANIC! Everyone makes bad decisions. Don't make excuses, take responsibility for screwing up and move forward. Without beating yourself up too much, analyze what went wrong and take stock for future reference. Make any apologies or explanations that you need to – don't make any that you don't need to.

It's very tempting to dwell on a poor decision and get swept up by negative thoughts – don't. Get your focus back on the present and move forward with a positive attitude. Adulting doesn't mean you're expected to get everything right all the time. You will make more bad decisions – everyone does – and learning how to be resilient and move on is one of life's great lessons.

NEGOTIATE
like a champ

**YOUR ADULTING GOAL
FOR THIS CHAPTER:**
*To learn the tools to negotiate like a grown-up
in a world where tantrums and throwing your
toys out the pram aren't winning tactics.*

One of the golden rules of parenting is not to negotiate with your
kids. What the parent says goes, and if you capitulate even just
once, well, you've lost all authority and the children run feral. No
wonder then that we reach adulthood unable to negotiate like a
champ — lots of practice trying to get an extra bag of sweets but
with ineffective skills. When negotiation is less about getting dad
to agree to an extra TV show before bed and more about getting
a pay rise, what do you need to be a winner?

GOLDEN RULES OF NEGOTIATION

Negotiation is a way of reaching an agreement or compromise
whilst avoiding conflict. Think of it as deciding who gets to buy
the next round of drinks, making sure it's not you whilst at the
same time keeping your friends. Try these rules where negotiation
is needed and there's no one there to hold your hand:

Always be the one to start the negotiations...

... that way you'll tend to be the one in control. Just think of that awkward moment when you walk towards someone and sidestep in the same direction like in an elaborate mating ritual. Be the one to stop sidestepping first and stride forward, and you'll be the one on your way fastest.

Know what you want

If you aren't clear in your head what you want, the predators across the table will smell your weakness. What is your strategy? ('Strategy' is a grown-up word you'll have to use a lot if you want to crack adulting.)

Keep cool

Keep a cool head – particularly if those around you are losing their composure. Letting off steam, venting anger and overly emotional behavior are not going to get you want you want – stick with calm and collected logic.

Be armed with information

Knowledge is power, someone very wise once said. Know your stuff and you're unlikely to be backfooted. Research is key, and is of course a very grown-up way to approach it. Save winging it for next time your mother calls to ask why you missed that important family meal.

What's your bargaining zone?

Know this before you start negotiating. What's the most you're willing to give up? What's the least you're willing to walk away with? That zone in between is where you'll be happiest with the outcome.

> ## "Everything is negotiable. Whether or not the negotiation is easy is another thing."
> CARRIE FISHER

Don't be rushed

If someone thinks you're in a hurry, they'll take advantage of that. Take your time and let the pressure build on the other side, and with any luck, they'll cave in rather than lose out completely.

Be prepared to walk away ...

... or to let the other person walk away. Don't settle on something you're not happy with. You're an adult now – hold your nerve and stand your ground!

STALEMATE

Negotiations have reached a deadlock. Now you're 'adulting', you can't toss a coin, wrestle for it or ask someone to decide for you. What should you do?

Is there something you could give in on (i.e. make the other side think they've won the battle – only you will know they've not won the war) that will make them give you what you want in return? Angle for something that's not important to them but that is really important to you.

Suggest a break. Go away and pummel a pillow, run around the block, eat a donut. Anything to give you a moment to gather your thoughts and morph back into adulting mode ready to take on the world.

HOW TO NEGOTIATE LIKE A CHILD

This is everything you *shouldn't* be doing. Unless of course you're negotiating with someone who is yet to master adulting to your level:

Throw a tantrum. Stick your fingers in your ears and say 'La la la'. Cry to get sympathy. Steal the other person's pen and refuse to give it back to them (or lick it before you give it back).

SOME PEOPLE ARE LIKE TREES, THEY TAKE FOREVER TO GROW UP.

Say no
AND MEAN IT

YOUR ADULTING GOAL FOR THIS CHAPTER:

To learn how to say no to something you don't want to do without feeling the need to lie, explain or worry about what people think of you. Time is precious, and if you're adulting like a boss, you need to focus on those things you really want to be doing.

Elton John once sang that 'sorry' seems to be the hardest word. In fact, 'no' is a very close contender when it comes to adulting. When we want to say 'no' we'll say everything but that, especially if we're asked a question in person:

- I'll check my calendar when I get home and text you (because texting means I won't have to tell you in person and you won't notice me blush as I lie).

- That sounds great, I'd love to come to your party (but I have no intention of turning up and I'll drop out via text a couple of hours before it starts).

- Yes, it's been ages! We must meet up, I'd love to catch up (but I'll make sure we never do because I don't like you all that much).

- The project sounds so interesting, let me check how I can fit it in (although I'd rather stick pins in my eyes than take it on).

TRICKS FOR SAYING NO

To adult like a boss, you need to learn subtlety and to read context – that is, how to say no according to your audience and when *not* to say no.

Your personal life

Unwanted nights out, second dates, that party when you just want to stay in – invitations in your personal life abound (lucky you) and you might be overwhelmed by peer pressure, but sometimes you're simply not interested. How can you say 'no' without being rude?

- Actually use the word 'no'! And say it fast – not couched amongst umming and ahing – so that you are clear and confident that you mean it.

- So as not to be rude, give some explanation but keep it short and sweet.

- Suggest an alternative – make it something you actually want to do!

At work

Saying 'no' at work can be uncomfortable – you're employed to do as you're told by your boss. The key is knowing when to push back. If you're already overloaded with work or you're being asked to complete something within an unrealistic timescale, consider what's best for your own mental health and for your employer.

You don't want to produce work that's below par because it was done too quickly or under unreasonable pressure. The task might not be within your job description, it could be completely unnecessary or conflict with your values. Know how to use this powerful two-letter word in a constructive way:

- Think before you give your answer. Would it help your career to say yes? Or would it be the straw that breaks the camel's back?

- Suggest an alternative when you say no. Could you help your colleague at a later date or assist with a smaller part in the meantime? Explain your current commitments and why you need to prioritize.

- Say no in person. The tone of an email is easily misinterpreted – what you intended as perfectly polite could be read by someone else as rude.

- What are the consequences of saying no? Adulting means you're responsible for your own actions. Make sure there are good reasons for saying no – or yes.

- If you've built your reputation as a conscientious employee, saying no for valid reasons once in a while won't be frowned upon – it'll enhance your integrity.

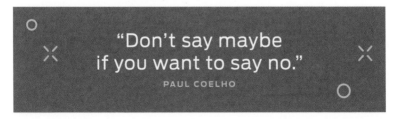

"Don't say maybe
if you want to say no."
PAUL COELHO

HELP! THEY WON'T TAKE NO FOR AN ANSWER!

By being firm and clear in your initial 'no', you should be able close down any opportunities to be persuaded otherwise. If a person won't accept your answer, whatever you do, don't cry like a toddler. Remember that it's not your business to make them happy, so stick to your guns and walk away. It's tough — we've been trained to be polite. Adulting means understanding that saying 'no' doesn't make you a bad person — it just makes you someone who said no this time.

A MIRACLE IS WHEN YOU SAY NO TO A GLASS OF WINE.

Getting the
JOB

Commiserations. It's a tough time to join the job market. And
if you're a supposedly pampered millennial, you won't get any
sympathy from the rest of the population. Without getting a job,
you can't be independent; but it's hard to get a job so you're still
living with your parents ... being a pampered millennial. Let's face
it, you can't win.

APPLY YOURSELF

You need a brilliant resumé to wow your potential employer.
Research shows that you only have 9 seconds to grab their
attention. You need to demonstrate quick smart that you'll be
great at the job and that you've got the maturity to be a fabulous
employee. So, don't include:

- Your hobbies. Reading, going to the cinema, eating out
  – these won't make you stand out from the hip crowd.

Painting Warhammer figures and role playing might make you stand out, but for all the wrong reasons.

■ Irrelevant work experience. No one cares about that after-school job you loved in the comic store.

■ Lies. It's not *if* but *when* you'll get found out, so use all your strength to resist what you think are job-winning porkies.

■ Spelling ~~misteaks~~ mistakes, grammatical errors or poor forMat*ting*. A sure-fire way for your resumé to hit the bin.

If you want to make a positive impact, include:

■ Information that's tailored to the job. If the job requires sales experience, make sure you flag up your skills in that area (employers will be looking for keywords), don't give space to your history of summer fruit picking.

■ Don't leave any gaps. Better to explain the employment gaps than to arouse the suspicions of your prospective employer. Even if you don't think a position is relevant to the job, include but just give minimum detail.

■ Be concise. Use bullet points. Have a no waffle rule! (Apparently Elon Musk's resumé fits on one page …).

■ Keep the format traditional and let the content speak for itself. The harder you try to stand out, the more likely it is to backfire. So, no purple paper or glitter in the envelope.

You might also want to clean up your social media presence before your resumé hits an employer's inbox. It's not uncommon for employers to check candidates online, so make sure you don't look like someone they wouldn't employ in a million years.

> ## "The road to success is lined with many tempting parking spaces."
> PROVERB

THE INTERVIEW

Well done! Your resumé must have been an awesome tribute to your adulting skills. Now it's time to polish your shoes and emerge from behind the safety of your keyboard. Here are 10 top tips for bossing your interview:

1. Research your potential employer to within an inch of its life. Fail to do so and you'll just look like, well, an idiot.

2. First impressions (see also page 36). Eye contact, a firm handshake, be spick and span like it's your first day of school and SMILE.

3. Know why you want the job. You'll be asked, so even if you need to big it up a little, be keen.

4. Don't wear novelty items. Socks, ties, waistcoats, earrings, etc., with cartoon characters on them are a huge no-no. You're a big boy/girl now.

5. Have some questions prepared (even if you know the answers). It'll make you look amazing, and of course, highly intelligent – as all grown-ups should be.

6. Be prepared for all the common interview questions: 'Tell us about yourself ... '; 'Where do you see yourself in 5 years?'; 'What are your strengths and weaknesses?' (see below).

7. If you've had a heavy night the previous night (which shouldn't have happened before an interview if you're adulting like a pro): DO NOT be late, DO NOT be miserable, moody or morose. Enthusiasm, enthusiasm, enthusiasm!

8. Compliment the company's work. Without being creepy.

9. Strike a balance between confidence and professionalism. Cockiness is a turn-off.

10. And if the nerves are really getting to you, remember the classic tactic of picturing your interviewers in their underwear.

WHAT ARE YOUR WEAKNESSES?

The famous interview question that *always* comes up. Don't say that you don't have any. Are you really that un-self-aware? Be ready for it.

Pick a weakness that's a strength in disguise, e.g. perfectionism (you put pressure on yourself to perform but it makes for high-quality work).

> "Never ruin an apology
> with an excuse."
> ANON

Pick a weakness then show how you can overcome it, e.g. you've not got much experience in this field but you're committed and a fast learner.

Keeping
YOUR JOB

**YOUR ADULTING GOAL
FOR THIS CHAPTER:**
*Simple: how to behave in a manner that
ensures you keep your job!*

Getting a job is an amazing achievement in a tough job market,
so you need to hang on to it with all your might. As long as you
play along with the rules of the workplace and remember to keep
adulting like a pro, you'll soon be the star employee.

THE TOP 10 BASICS YOU NEED TO KNOW

These are the basics for adulting in the workplace. If any come as
a surprise to you, be a little bit ashamed but then crack on.

1. Be punctual. Including not leaving before you're supposed to.

2. Adhere to dress codes. Especially what levels you can and
    can't strip down to in the summer.

3. Attitude! A bad attitude will have you out the door in a flash.
    Keep it positive.

4. Work hard. Do what you're paid to be there to do. It's not a
    free internet café.

5. Work as a team – even if you can't stand some of your colleagues.

6. Work events – not the time to show off how much you can drink.

7. Keep work and social media separate.

8. Be flexible. No one likes a jobsworth so go the extra mile, even if it's out of your remit.

9. Don't get involved in arguments about who has stolen someone's lunch from the office refrigerator. Certainly don't stick confrontational notes on the 'fridge door.

10. Grin and bear it. Maybe it's not the job of your dreams but it's a job – make the best of it whilst you plan your next move.

MAKE YOURSELF INDISPENSABLE

No one is really indispensable – but you can make a darned good stab at trying to be. What makes you so valuable that you'd be the last person to be asked to leave the building? Knowledge, for starters. Become the go-to person with knowledge on a certain area that other people don't have. You can acquire this knowledge by working on high-profile projects (which also get you 'seen'), or if certain skills in your team are lacking, get yourself trained

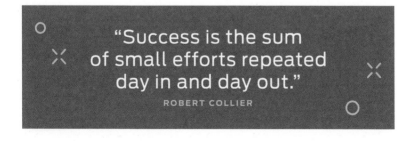

"Success is the sum of small efforts repeated day in and day out."
ROBERT COLLIER

in them and become the guru. Whatever you do, make sure it reflects the priorities and goals of your boss and the company — be seen to be contributing to success (and claim some of it!)

DESK ETIQUETTE

Remember that your desk says something about your personality and that some items will put a dent in your professional image:

- Cuddly toys (particularly if you line them up along the top of your monitor).

- Inappropriate photos of your last mates' holiday in the hottest clubbing destination.

- Leftover food. Enough said.

- Inspirational quotes that aren't, well, inspirational (especially if they include swear words).

- A crazy number of post-it notes that make it look like you don't know if you're coming or going.

WHEN YOU WANT TO GO OUT BUT YOU'VE GOT WORK NEXT DAY:

FRIEND: I'LL MEET YOU AT ABOUT 10? ME: AT NIGHT?

TIME,
precious time

As you fill your life with adulting tasks then you might start to feel
like you have less time for the fun stuff. Not true. It's just about
learning to manage your time effectively. If you're letting your
laundry pile up whilst playing video games, you're not winning at
being a grown-up. That pile of dirty clothes isn't going anywhere,
it's only growing. Deal with it.

BASICS OF TIME MANAGEMENT

These may sound like they're falling straight out of the mouth
of a middle manager, but take heed as they apply to both work
and play:

- **Set your goals:** What do you want/need to do? By when?
  By having something to aim for you can focus on the task
  in hand and ignore what doesn't contribute to your goal.
  Getting distracted by a TV show whilst you're on the way
  to get the vacuum cleaner isn't going to get last night's
  popcorn out of the rug.

- **Prioritize:** Are you doing the most pressing job first? Or are you procrastinating and just doing the easiest one – or nothing at all? Think about whether the task in hand is contributing to your goal. And if you find yourself arranging your book collection by color, ask yourself: 'Why am I doing this?'

- **Know when to say 'no':** If something's unnecessary or doesn't contribute to your goal, you've a valid reason to say a big fat 'no'. (See *Say No and Mean It*, page 21.)

- **Make a to-do list:** Get it out your head and onto paper. Make adulting fun by using different colored highlighters to prioritize tasks. Go really crazy with multi-colored post-its if that's what makes it work for you.

- **Do tougher tasks when you're at your most productive:** If you're a morning person, make that tricky job the first thing you tackle. Save more routine jobs that don't need much brain power for when you hit the mid-afternoon slump.

- **Distraction:** Step away from the smart phone. Disable the internet. Tell your mother to call you later. Being distracted by people, things, eyebrow plucking, etc., will make even the quickest job take forever. Focus, do one thing at once, ignore pings in your inbox and you'll be well on the way to getting the job done.

WOOHOO – FREE TIME!

Great, you've tackled your jobs like a grown-up. That pile of laundry has vanished, you've got food in the refrigerator and your boss is off your back as you've met the deadline. So, what do you do with all the wonderful free time you've got? You have two options:

1. **Totally waste it**. That's right – WASTE IT. We all need complete downtime every so often to recharge our mental and physical batteries. What's your favorite waste of time? It could be a long lie-in, building Lego or bingeing on a box set. Do it, enjoy it and don't feel guilty. If it's doing you good, then actually it's not a waste of time at all.

2. **Don't waste it**. Don't choose Option 1 if it leaves you wishing you were doing something else. Confused? Don't be. For example, don't lie in bed if it's simply because you can't be bothered to get up rather than because you enjoy it. That's a bad waste of time. If you've got hobbies you love, places you want to go or people you want to see, you have to make the time. Use your spare time wisely – it should contribute to something even if it's just to give you a minor sense of achievement.

> "The bad news is time flies.
> The good news is
> you're the pilot."
> MICHAEL ALTSHULER

Great first
IMPRESSIONS

**YOUR ADULTING GOAL
FOR THIS CHAPTER:**
*To understand that first impressions matter
in the world of adulting and how you can
make yours great.*

Surely when you're a grown-up you can worry less about what
people think? Yes ... and no. Even if you're old enough to feel
comfortable in your own skin, there's a fine line to be trod
between not caring what other people think of you and making a
good impression.

MAKING AN IMPRESSION
– WHAT NOT TO DO

■ **Try too hard:** Stand out by all means – just remember
that there are bad ways of being memorable if you try
too hard. There's plenty of time for revealing the 'real
you' when you've a better idea of what your audience
can handle.

■ **Be exhausting**: Talking over people, not listening,
interrupting and filling every gap in the conversation
with inane drivel isn't going to help you make friends
and influence people.

- **Assume others hold the same views as you**: Talking politics or expressing very strong opinions when you don't know people well is guaranteed to make you stick in their minds for all the wrong reasons.

- **Check your phone mid conversation**: The height of modern rudeness. Don't do it.

- **Avoid eye contact**: Just plain shifty. What are you hiding? Make it even worse by **not smiling**.

- **Arrive late without a very, very good reason**: Shows a lack of interest and respect.

MAKING A QUICK RECOVERY

You've really screwed up. How can you redeem yourself? Don't panic – is it as bad as you imagine? It's all too easy to catastrophize. Try these tactics to turn around the person you failed to impress.

Surprise them – show a different side to yourself that contradicts the bad impression. Don't avoid them – if you hide yourself away, how can you change their opinion of you? Apologize – then let it

> "If you want to make a good first impression, smile at people. What does it cost to smile? Nothing."
> GUY KAWASAKI

go as over-apologizing just gets annoying. Ask for their advice – flattery is a powerful thing. Persist – it can take time to change a bad impression but don't give up.

But remember, you don't need to get along with everyone. Are they actually worth worrying about? Sometimes, life really is just too short.

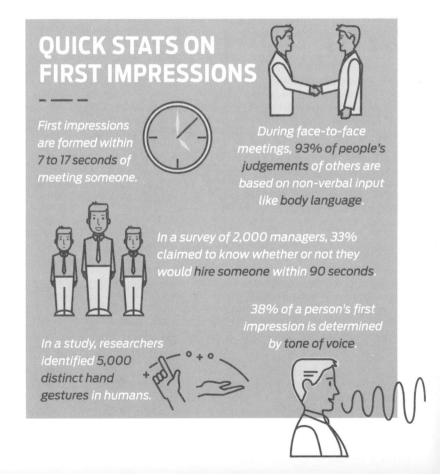

QUICK STATS ON FIRST IMPRESSIONS

First impressions are formed within 7 to 17 seconds of meeting someone.

During face-to-face meetings, 93% of people's judgements of others are based on non-verbal input like body language.

In a survey of 2,000 managers, 33% claimed to know whether or not they would hire someone within 90 seconds.

38% of a person's first impression is determined by tone of voice.

In a study, researchers identified 5,000 distinct hand gestures in humans.

All in the
PRESENTATION

**YOUR ADULTING GOAL
FOR THIS CHAPTER:**
*Learn how to present well in social and work
situations so that no one guesses you feel like
a 12-year-old in a grown-up's body.*

The world can be an unforgiving place for grown-ups. It's
assumed that you're big and ugly enough to know how to present
with confidence in any given situation. But for many people, giving
a presentation fills them with horror. You're laying yourself bare
before the eyes of others – will they discover you're an imposter?

HOW TO NAIL A PRESENTATION

■ **Slides – a slippery slope:** It's tempting to use lots of
slides to deflect people's eyes off you – don't. (And don't
use crazy PowerPoint effects unless you're presenting to
school kids – totally unprofessional.) Being able to talk
without reading through your slides is incredibly engaging.
People will listen better and, inspired by your confidence,
will buy in to what you're saying.

■ **Entertain**: You're there to breathe life into a subject so
give it some oomph – otherwise you might as well just
circulate a handout and wait quietly at the front for any

questions. Even insurance and macroeconomics can be fascinating if you find a story to tell and connect people.

- **Don't rush it**: If your audience feels you rushing and can't hear the message through your nerves, they'll want to get to the end just as much as you do.

- **Make eye contact** with everyone in the room. Don't freak out if you see anyone scowling — there's always one who's not had their coffee.

- **Project!** But don't shout. You want people to hear you, not cower in their seats. Stand tall and let the air fill your lungs. And pause for breath.

- **Practice** until you're sick of the sound of your own voice. Practice might not make perfect when you throw nerves into the mix, but at least you'll know it's all up there in your head (you just need to get it out of your mouth).

- **If you feel an 'um' or an 'err' coming on**, simply pause and take a breath in.

FIELD A QUESTION YOU DON'T KNOW THE ANSWER TO WITHOUT LOOKING LIKE AN IDIOT

Don't panic and immediately say 'I don't know' (or wave goodbye to your credibility). These responses will get you out of a hole:

- "I don't have enough information to answer your question fully, but I will take it away and look into it." (Keep your promise by sending a follow-up email to attendees.)

> **"If you're presenting yourself with confidence, you can pull off pretty much anything."**
> KATY PERRY

- Redirect the question and tell them what you do know. (Obviously it needs to be in some way connected to the question so it doesn't look like you're avoiding it completely.)

- Ask the audience (sounding interested rather than desperate): "Can anyone help answer that question?"

Whatever you do, don't fake it. People can spot that from a mile away and you'll look like an immature and naïve child (which you may be, but you don't want people to know that).

BODY TALK

Powerful body language will make both you and your audience believe you're grown-up and responsible enough to be presenting important information. Here's a quick guide to making body language your friend in presentations:

- Make eye contact with everyone – you might be surprised who the decision-makers are.

- Don't slouch. Chest out and shoulders back – this will help you breathe more easily too.

- Allow yourself to gesture naturally. Don't plan the best parts to wave your arms around in – that'll just look daft and contrived.

- Keep it visually interesting and walk around. You're not a tree so don't be rooted to the spot.

- Use positive gestures like smiling and nodding and you'll win over your audience.

**PRESENTATIONS:
THE GROWN-UP
VERSION OF
SHOW AND TELL.**

How to make
SMALL TALK

Have you ever been dragged away from a conversation in the
street by your child? Have you endured a shopping trip with your
mother where she bumped into everyone she's ever known since
kindergarten? Then you'll know what a big part small talk plays
in the lives of grown-ups, whether we like it or not.

WHAT'S SMALL TALK?

Small talk is polite conversation about unimportant matters. It's
important that the topics aren't controversial. You wouldn't meet
a first date with the line: "I'm Jane. Lovely to meet you. I'm all
for building a wall around the whole of the country." That would
entirely defeat the objective of well-mannered chit-chat.

WHY BOTHER WITH SMALL TALK?

It's a social nicety – and a necessary evil. It's a gentle approach
to meeting someone for the first time and you're trying to be

moderately interesting whilst tiptoeing around topics that might offend. Small talk is perfect for filling awkward gaps in conversations both with people you know well or complete strangers.

SAFE SMALL TALK TOPICS

- The weather

- Vacation destinations

- Family

- Sport and hobbies

- Work

- Which school you went to

- Celebrities (if you want to be really shallow).

HELP! I'M TERRIBLE AT SMALL TALK!

Never fear, it's doesn't always come naturally but you can learn to get better at it. Try these tips for getting over the social awkwardness:

1. Have a list of potential conversation topics in your head. Read the papers for any interesting stories – but make sure they're not too juvenile (remember, you're adulting!) or controversial.

2. Listen like your life depends on it. You'll pick up cues about what excites your companion that will help you keep the small talk going. Show you're listening – nod, smile, insert

> ○ "I'm not good at small talk;
> ✕ I'm not good at big talk;
> and medium talk just
> doesn't come up."
>
> AMY HEMPEL ○

noises of encouragement – don't check your phone while they talk or you'll look up to find them gone.

3. Ask questions – you'll need to be doing number 2 above to be able to do this. Random questions suggest you're not listening. Relevant questions win you mega brownie points. Everyone loves to think that what they're saying is interesting, so reinforce that even if their vacation story is as dull as dishwater.

4. Don't fear silence. It's useful for letting you catch a breath and to process your thoughts. A break in the conversation is normal so don't feel pressured to fill the silence. It may be a sign that it's time to move on to a new topic. Or revert to an earlier topic and say: "I was really interested in what you were saying about XXXX – tell me more ...".

5. Body language is important. How you hold yourself can make the other person feel more relaxed. If you're clenching your jaw or jiggling, your nerves will transfer to them (or they'll back away slowly ...). Keep your shoulders relaxed, face the person you're chatting to and keep regular eye contact. And don't cross your arms – the classic defensive posture! You're not there for a fight.

FINANCIAL
adulting

YOUR ADULTING GOAL FOR THIS CHAPTER:

The big one. Planning and managing your finances. Without doing this you're forever destined to be a child, dependent on others. Don't put it off, sort it out. Here are the basics of what you need to know.

What are the foundations for your financial success? It's not the most scintillating of topics but it is one of the most important if you're going to fully embrace adulting and emerge into accountable maturity.

- **Know where your money goes**. Keep track of what you're spending and the bills going out of your bank account. Adults know this as BUDGETING.

- **Save**. It's really hard to do if you're just starting out on your adulting journey, but if you can save even a tiny amount each month – do it. A little bit set aside is a must for those emergency situations like your washing machine dying or a new games console being released ...

- **Exercise self-control!** Yes, the last line about the games console was a joke. The key to keeping money in your pocket is – you've guessed it – not spending it on raindrops on roses and whiskers on kittens. And resist buying your favorite things on credit – show you're a responsible adult by saving for something before you buy it. Adults know this as DEFERRED GRATIFICATION. (Not as sexy as it sounds.)

TAXES

A confusing minefield that thankfully your employer will deal with the brunt of. However, understanding taxes will allow you to talk with the grown-ups at frightfully dull dinner parties and, more importantly, to budget your money. Will the income taxes being deducted from the salary of the job you've been offered leave you with enough to cover all your living costs? Depending on which country you live in, taxes can hit your bottom line hard, so know thy enemy.

INSURANCE

Health insurance. Homeowner's insurance. Car insurance. Life insurance. Pet insurance. Phone insurance. Insurance insurance. Don't be dazzled by everyone wanting to make money from

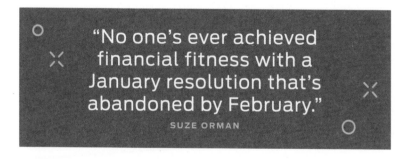

"No one's ever achieved financial fitness with a January resolution that's abandoned by February."
SUZE ORMAN

your fears. The key insurance policies you need are: health, homeowner's/renter's, car, life and disability (protection if you're unable to work) insurance. Make good use of online comparison sites to find the best price but don't scrimp on the coverage.

PENSIONS

Scariest of all – pensions are a reminder that you're going to get old. You need to start saving for your retirement as soon as possible to have any chance of a comfortable retirement. Sad but brutally true. So, it's never too early to think beyond adulting and into old-ageing. Know how much you need to save to retire comfortably – what % of your salary do you need to save to retire in XX years?

DEBTS

Building up debts is inevitable. Costs of education, setting up home, even just buying clothes for your first job can set you back. The important thing is to keep debt under control and to seek help quickly if it starts to become unmanageable. Pay off debt as quickly as you can (if it's a small amount) or regularly and steadily (if it's a larger sum). Keep your credit card balance as low as possible. Exercise that self-control mentioned above. And most of all, get over that mentality you had as a child that money on cards or out of ATMs is free! No money is free – debt will firmly bite you on your grown-up behind if you don't keep it in check.

SIMPLE MONEY SAVING (AND EARNING) TIPS

- Make use of online comparison sites to compare the best prices for financial products.

- Before spending money, ask: Do I need it? Can I afford it? Can I find it cheaper elsewhere?

- Don't touch payday loans with a barge pole – they can be a nightmare.

- Simple things like switching off lights and not leaving taps running will save money on energy and utility bills.

- Get rid of the things you don't need. Sell them online.

- Drop one brand level when buying groceries.

- Be bold and haggle! You don't need to accept the first price.

If financial adulting is all a bit too much for you, don't just stick your head in the sand. Speak to a friend or family member who's already got adulting nailed and get their advice. If you're really stuck, then see a professional financial advisor.

HOME
sweet home

YOUR ADULTING GOAL
FOR THIS CHAPTER:

*Get the lowdown on entering the property
market and how to home own like a
responsible adult.*

If you've bought your own home, congratulations! You've well and
truly joined the grown-up world. Unless you've won the lottery,
inherited a fortune or have VERY generous parents, becoming a
homeowner will have been a tough road. Take a moment to pat
yourself on the back. But the journey doesn't end there. There's a
whole closet or garage worth of gadgets and tools that you need
to own, not forgetting the insurance policies and bills ...

If you're thinking of buying your first home, good luck! Here's
hoping you've thought it all through — but more of that at the end
of the chapter.

NEW HOMEOWNER CHECKLIST

Now you have to rely on yourself rather than your parents, be
prepared for the practical stuff that homeowning entails:

- Have you got all the right insurance in place? This is
  something that you should NEVER forget or scrimp on.

- Check security. Do you need to beef up the locks or install motion sensor lighting outside? (Also check the minimum levels of security required by your home insurance.)

- Think about maintenance. It could be cleaning the gutters or keeping an unruly garden under control. Taking time for regular maintenance will save you money in the long run.

- Do you know how to shut off gas, water and electricity in an emergency? Don't leave locating the shut-off valve until you're stemming the flood from a burst pipe.

- Throw a housewarming party ...

BE MASTER OF YOUR BILLS

Adulting means facing a flurry of bills and maintaining a calm face whilst inside you're panicking at the mere sight of an envelope. The key is to not let them master you:

- Pay your bills automatically from your bank account. Not only will you not forget to pay them, there's often a discount available for this payment method.

- Shop around for the best prices for energy and insurance, etc. Negotiate and haggle as there's usual some slack a company will cut you if they're keen to keep your business.

> "The best time to buy a home is always five years ago."
>
> RAY BROWN

- If you're struggling to pay a bill, face it like a grown-up (don't hide like a child). Speak to the company before the debt spirals.

- If you can, keep an emergency fund set aside for any unexpected bills. Roof repairs and broken heating systems have no respect for struggling homeowners.

HIGH MAINTENANCE

Unless you're adept in a relevant trade like building or plumbing, owning your own home is going to be a DIY learning curve. Yes, maybe you can call on your parents to help, but at some point you're going to have to take responsibility for looking after your home all on your lonesome. The internet is an absolute godsend for instructional how-to videos on every imaginable DIY task. Look into evening courses at local colleges too and save yourself the cost of employing a professional.

Here's the basic toolkit every homeowner needs: hammer (and some nails), tape measure, spirit level, wrench, pliers, drill, screwdrivers (a flat head and a Phillips). That should get you started, but be prepared for your collection to grow as you tweak and fix your home.

TO BUY OR TO RENT?

If you've not yet bought your own home but everyone around you is, it's tempting to feel peer pressure. But the big decision to buy a property has to be right for you. Are you ready?

- Can you afford it? Work out how much the monthly cost of owning your home would be compared to renting (including mortgage, insurance, taxes, bills).

WHEN YOU NEED TO CLIMB YOUR TRASH TO GET OUT THE DOOR.

- Do you have the money for a down payment/deposit? If not, it might be better to take time to save rather than borrow it.

- What are your long-term goals? If you dream of travelling the world in a year's time, is the cost of home ownership going to allow you to save the money you need?

AND IF YOU DO DECIDE TO BUY ...

Listen to all the advice you can, especially from friends who've recently bought. Tricks and tips are the way to survive a competitive (and sometimes brutal) market.

- Know when you've got a good realtor/agent. The good 'uns won't try to sell you something way out of your price range, they'll keep in contact with regular updates and they'll get you in to properties before they're advertised.

- Start saving. Buying and moving is an expensive business. Also check out your credit score and improve it if need be.

- Think carefully about the area you want to live in and why. And think about the future, not just whether there's a good bar around the corner for next Saturday night. If you're planning a family, do you want to be near grandparents and good schools?

- Have a list of 'must have' features and those you can compromise on. This will help you sift through the properties available.

> "Sometimes I lie awake at night, and ask, 'Where have I gone wrong?' Then a voice says to me, 'This is going to take more than one night.'"
>
> **CHARLES M. SCHULZ**

Give something
BACK

**YOUR ADULTING GOAL
FOR THIS CHAPTER:**
*To get to grips with the fact that there's a
bigger world out there than just yours, and if
you're in the position to help others, that's the
responsible thing to do.*

Millennials – or indeed anyone trying to leap the chasm into
adulthood – get a lot of bad press about their supposed
selfishness and sense of entitlement. However, research shows
that they're much more socially and environmentally conscious
than previous generations. Take that naysayers!

BIGGING UP THE MILLENNIALS

Here's what they're already doing better than the generations
before them:

▪ Purchasing sustainably sourced products.

▪ Corporate social responsibility – including challenging
unethical practices in the workplace.

▪ Making social good part of their everyday activities.

WHY SHOULD YOU GIVE SOMETHING BACK?

If you're not already rocking your moral compass, here are just a few reasons why you should be:

- Every day, approximately 8 million pieces of plastic pollution find their way into the world's oceans.

- 10.9% of the world is living on less than $2 a day.

- For every 1,000 children born, 41 will die before they turn 5 years old.

- On average, people in the United States are expected to live 18 years longer than people born in Sub-Saharan Africa.

- Due mainly to habitat loss, we've lost 60% of wild vertebrates since 1970.

Sobering, isn't it? Part of adulting is taking responsibility for changing things. But don't flinch at the word 'responsibility' – you don't need to shoulder the world's woes all by yourself. Make small changes, give small amounts: it's not the size that matters, it's the fact that you care at all. Donate, volunteer, help campaigns go viral on social media – do something.

> "As you grow older, you will discover that you have two hands – one for helping yourself, the other for helping others."
>
> AUDREY HEPBURN

RECEIVING POST AS A KID: YAY! I CAN'T WAIT TO SEE WHAT I'VE GOT – AMAZING!

RECEIVING POST AS AN ADULT: OH NO – HOW MUCH DO I OWE THIS TIME?

START LOCAL

It's not just globally where you can make a difference, you need to think local too. Some great ways to start:

- **Volunteer your time** and see first-hand the difference you're making. It could be a homeless shelter, a food bank, a community center, or an animal shelter.

- **Pitch up to local fundraising events**. Small local charities put lots of effort into fundraising events to keep their cause going. Volunteer to help or simply attend, spend some money and show your support.

- **Use your social media accounts to spread the word**. Is a charity asking for donations? Do they need help at an event? Tell your friends and family about it and harness the power of the medium you usually only use for selfies.

How to
EMBRACE FAILURE

No one likes failure. If you can learn to deal with it in a grown-up way and manage the inevitable stress around it, there are all kinds of positive benefits both to you and how you're perceived by those around you.

RESILIENCE

Resilience is the ability to recover quickly when things go wrong. It's how well you adapt to events and adversity in your life. The more resilience you have, the easier you'll find it to bounce back. In fact, it's an essential skill for coping with life's challenges. Can you improve your resilience? Yes. The foundation of resilience is good emotional and physical wellbeing so if you're not already, now's the time to start looking after yourself. See the chapter on Self-care, page 76.

POSITIVE APPROACHES TO FAILURE

If you can learn how to deal with failure in a healthy way, you'll become a lot less scared of failing another time:

■ It's okay to feel bad for a bit. Acknowledge your feelings. By doing that, you'll work through them and realize that you can beat them now and again in the future if you need to.

■ Replace negative thoughts with positive ones. Rather than think 'I've failed at this — I'm useless', say 'This hasn't gone as I'd hoped this time, but I've learnt how to make it work next time'.

■ Talk! Have a strong network of people around you who you can confide in. Getting someone else's thoughts can put things in perspective. What might seem like a terrible failure in your mind is probably viewed entirely differently by those around you.

■ What are your favorite ways to relax? A long bath, a new novel, breathing exercises? Use these to reduce your stress levels and you'll be in a better state of mind to move forward.

■ Adulting is all about accepting responsibility. When something goes wrong, make sure you accept an *appropriate* level of responsibility. Don't beat yourself up if the failure was caused by something outside of your control.

> "Success is not final, failure is not fatal: it is the courage to continue that counts."
> WINSTON CHURCHILL

- Don't see failure as a step backwards, see it as an opportunity to move forward having learnt something and grown wiser.

FAMOUS 'FAILURES'

Charles Darwin dropped out of school … twice. Now considered one of the most influential scientific minds ever.

John Grisham's first book was rejected by publishers 28 times.

Sir James Dyson made over 5,000 failed prototypes before he produced the first successful Dyson vacuum.

Walt Disney was fired from a newspaper job because he lacked imagination!

Stephen Spielberg was rejected from film school … THREE times.

J. K. Rowling, a nearly penniless single parent, went from depending on welfare to being one of the richest women in the world in only five years.

Thomas Edison made 1,000 unsuccessful attempts at inventing the light bulb.

Beethoven's music teacher told his parents that he was too stupid to be a composer.

Henry Ford's early businesses failed, leaving him broke five times. He was told not to get into automobile manufacturing because he didn't know enough about it.

Think how different the world would've been had these famous people let failure get the better of them and given up!

ADMITTING
you're wrong ...

YOUR ADULTING GOAL FOR THIS CHAPTER:
Learn how to swallow your pride and admit you're wrong without weaseling out of it.

Responsibility is a scary word when you're used to all the freedom that being a child brings. Gone are the days when it was easy to blame the broken vase on your younger brother or to insist that you were absolutely not cheating at the board game (when clearly you were). Mistakes are hard to digest, but by admitting you're wrong and exposing a weakness, you're showing how strong you are. So:

- assume responsibility
- accept the consequences
- make it right
- say you're sorry.

WHAT NOT TO SAY ...

If you're admitting you're wrong, you're doing an amazing thing. Don't spoil it by undoing all your hard work with an ambiguous or barbed comment. For example, don't say:

- **The accusatory admission:** I got it wrong, but I didn't go on about it last time you did something wrong.

- **The pig-headed admission:** I'm sorry I got it wrong – I'm usually always right.

- **The empty admission:** I made a mistake. I said I made a mistake, alright?

WHAT YOU SHOULD SAY ...

Be truthful and sincere. Keep eye contact (or you'll look shifty) and don't smile (or you won't be taken seriously):

- **The constructive admission:** I've made a mistake, but I know how to fix it right away.

- **The humble admission:** I got that completely wrong, I took my eye off the ball.

- **The promise-to-do-better admission:** I really messed that up. It won't happen again.

ADULTING IS JUST EMAILING BACK AND FORWARD SAYING "SORRY FOR NOT GETTING BACK TO YOU" UNTIL ONE OF YOU DIES.

Saying you're
SORRY

No one likes to apologize, and it usually needs to be forced out
of us. It's painful — no wonder we're so reluctant to utter such a
short word. As a child, you're likely to get away with just an 'I'm
sorry for [eating the dog's food/drinking grandma's sherry/letting
the handbrake off in the car, etc.]' or simply a snorted one-word
apology. As an adult, it's much more complicated (because
apparently when you reach adulthood, you suddenly become
more eloquent and comfortable with difficult conversations …).

Remember the 3 Rs:

- **Responsibility**: Accept responsibility for what's
happened.

- **Regret**: Properly and directly apologize for what you've
done and the impact it had.

- **Redemption**: Think of what you can do to fix it or stop it
happening again.

If you're not sincere, you might as well not bother. It's vital you swallow your pride and throw yourself wholeheartedly into an apology. A good apology means laying yourself bare. And remember, forgiveness isn't automatic – it's entirely up to the other person, so don't pout if your perfectly acceptable apology is snubbed.

MISTAKES TO AVOID ...

The empty or incomplete apology: A sorry that accepts responsibility but doesn't touch on regret or redemption – "I'm sorry about this."

The OTT self-centered apology: Accepts responsibility but focuses on how the person apologizing feels, not what they've done wrong – "I'm really really sorry! I feel so awful! What a mess. I can't believe it's happened."

The argumentative apology: Simultaneously apologizes and retracts sole responsibility – "I'm sorry, but ...".

Finally, don't apologize for your intentions rather than the impact. Don't say "I didn't mean to ..." or "I'm sorry if ..." – acknowledge the effect of what you've done by saying "I'm sorry *that* ...". And keep those 3 Rs firmly in mind.

WHEN NOT TO APOLOGIZE

You should apologize when it's the right thing to do. Pause and think whether you've actually done anything that warrants an apology. If the answer is no, you don't need to apologize (or you completely lack self-awareness!). And never apologize for someone else's actions even if you're feeling bad through association.

Difficult
CONVERSATIONS

**YOUR ADULTING GOAL
FOR THIS CHAPTER:**
*Learn how to have a challenging conversation
without curling up in embarrassment or
blurting it out like a surly child.*

Everyone hates a difficult conversation. Whether it be telling
someone that their zipper is undone or that you've accidentally
run over their family pet, it's hard to find the right words. As a
child, you may have been blunt to the point of rudeness, devoid
of the social filters that adulthood brings. Those social filters are
crucial to adulting – they provide your sensitivity to the feelings of
others, even if inside you're cringing like a child.

HOW TO BROACH A TRICKY TOPIC

Don't put it off, but make sure you do choose the right time. If
you're dreading a conversation, it's tempting to postpone it – i.e.
avoid it. Only postpone it until the right time. Find a time when
there aren't other distractions, so no breaking up with a partner
whilst driving.

Don't imagine how the conversation will go. You'll imagine the
worst-case scenario, and if you do, you might never get around to

that conversation. If you approach it well, the outcome may be less stressful than you think.

What can you do to make it less upsetting? Think about ways to soften the blow (you need to put your sensitive hat on here). Is there an angle you can take that draws in something positive? But beware of being patronizing.

Come to the conversation calm. Having a conversation when you or the other person is angry or distressed is not going to produce a good outcome. Wait for emotions to settle before talking.

WHEN YOU'RE NOT ADULT ENOUGH YET TO SUPPORT ANYONE ELSE:

ME COMFORTING A FRIEND, "WOULD SOME HARIBO CHEER YOU UP?"

> "Listening well is one of the most powerful skills you can bring to a difficult conversation."
>
> DOUGLAS STONE

Launch straight into it. Don't start a difficult conversation with small talk about last night's big game. It sends the wrong message and delays the inevitable.

Prepare. Know what you want to say. Anticipate what the other person might say. And remember, honesty is the best policy.

And **don't do it over email or text message**! You're an adult now, not a teenager dumping a boy/girlfriend after two dates.

DON'T SAY:

- "It's not personal" – it almost certainly is.

- "I've only got a few minutes …" – an awful get-out clause on your part and suggests that the other person isn't very important.

- "I'm sorry you feel that way" – a horrible apology that's not an apology.

- "This is going to be difficult" – clearly you mean it's difficult for you!

DO SAY:

"I know what I'm about to say might not be easy to hear, but it's really important that we talk about this."

It's not
ALL ABOUT YOU

YOUR ADULTING GOAL
FOR THIS CHAPTER:
To understand the power of empathy, and the responsibility that you have as an adult to use it for good.

If you've been accused of not acting like a grown-up, it's likely that they also thought you were selfish, meaning you lack consideration for other people and are only concerned with your own personal profit or pleasure. Sounds familiar? If yes, then it's time to pull your socks up – you can't win at adulting with that attitude.

EMBRACE EMPATHY

Empathy is your ability to understand and share the feelings of others. If you struggle to understand why your best friend is devasted that her boyfriend cheated on her and to imagine how she's feeling, then you have some work to do. Good news is that empathy is a skill that you can learn, so there's really no excuse not to add it to your adulting toolbox.

WHY DOES THE WORLD NEED EMPATHY?

The modern world can be a scary place. Sometimes we might want to curl up in a fetal position and just hide, but being an adult and the responsibilities it brings with it means we can't do that. What you can do is bring empathy to the world – the more you understand, relate to and trust other people and encourage compassion, the better place the world will be. A little bit of kindness can go a very long way – you may even change the world.

BE MORE EMPATHETIC – TOP TIPS

- **Listen up**. Try to listen more than you speak and don't interrupt. Don't just look like you're listening – a couple of nods won't do – actively listen, which means *really hearing* and being able to ask intelligent questions.

- **Don't make assumptions**. To empathize with another person, you need to put your own preconceptions aside and step into their shoes.

- **Recognize the importance of the person's feelings**. Verbally acknowledge their anger or sadness, never tell them to just 'relax' or 'man up'.

- **Don't rush the conversation**. You might be feeling uncomfortable and keen to get away, but if you rush, the other person won't get the chance to express all their feelings. They'll end up feeling just as bad, and you'll be none the wiser about what you can do to help.

- **Ask questions**. Asking questions encourages the other person to share more. The more you can find out, the better able you are to provide practical and emotional support.

How not to be
GROSS

**YOUR ADULTING GOAL
FOR THIS CHAPTER:**
*Not sure whether breaking wind is acceptable
in all social situations? Find out what to do
and what not to do if you want to retain any
credibility.*

Rude, coarse and vulgar things are hilarious in childhood, and for
most people, they continue to raise a giggle in adulthood – but to
win at adulting you need to understand that there's a time and a
place. Things that make other people say "yuck" should generally
be avoided unless you know your audience is a like-minded one.

STOP THESE GROSS HABITS NOW

- Keep your phone and
keyboard clean. A square
inch of your phone harbors
around 25,000 germs. Your
toilet seat is cleaner. Think on
that next time you take a call
or type an email.

- Plugholes. Hair. Urgh. Either
buy a cheap gadget to

catch the hair or clean out
the plughole regularly. You
wouldn't tolerate it in the
showers at the gym, so why
tolerate it at home?

- The courtesy flush. Whether
you're sharing a bathroom
at home or at work, no
one wants to share your

emissions. Flush ASAP (you don't need to be completely finished) to minimize the noxious fumes.

■ Deodorant on dirty armpits really doesn't do the job you imagine it will. If you can't shower, at least wipe with a wet (clean) flannel before using your deodorant.

■ Toenail clippings are never acceptable. A partner should never have to extract your clippings from the soles of their feet.

■ Not changing your bedclothes for weeks on end. Think of the sweat, the dead skin cells and other bodily fluids that may knowingly or unknowingly escape.

■ We're all for ditching single-use plastic bottles but you've got to keep your reusable bottle clean. It can grow mold. Yes, really.

■ Picking your nose and eating it or wiping it somewhere. Just keep your fingers out of your nose in company. Private picks should be truly private — remember your car isn't a secret refuge and your boss/partner of your dreams may pull up next to you whilst you're busy with your nose.

TOP TRUMPS

Bodily eruptions are simultaneously funny and gross, and none more so than breaking wind. Apparently, there are 150 different words for bottom burps: farting, trumping, tooting, parping, letting one go being just a few of them. Booty belches are a universal human experience and know no borders. (Perhaps they could be the secret to world peace?) Whilst it's human to do a trouser cough, it's not always appropriate and might not warrant a high-five. This should be central to your understanding of adulting. If in doubt, hold it in.

SWIPE LEFT:
social media

**YOUR ADULTING GOAL
FOR THIS CHAPTER:**
*Understand how to behave on the internet
without having to delete your social media
accounts.*

Social media – Twitter, Facebook, Instagram, etc., etc., etc. –
have pretty much taken over the world. If you're not on social
media these days, you're making more of a statement than if you
are. When did it stop being fun and become a measure of self-
esteem? Remember, social media shows you everything through
a filter – don't be conned by how wonderful everyone else's lives
look. Keep it real.

SOCIAL MEDIA NO-NOS

Don't let yourself down with these social media faux pas:

- Too many selfies. So last year. So vain.

- Don't 'like' EVERYTHING you see. It makes you look like a
  stalker.

- Don't post anything that you'd be embarrassed for your
  grandma to see. An oldie but a goodie (the advice, not
  your grandma).

■ Oversharing. There's a long list of things that other people don't want to know about you. Your sex life and bodily functions just for starters. And no one is less interested in your cat than the rest of the world.

■ Stop inviting people to join in online games with you. It's annoying and shows you have nothing adult to fill your time with.

■ No one likes an internet bully or troll. If you can't say anything nice, don't say it at all.

■ Remember that your employer may be able to see what you post. If you can't resist laying yourself bare online, nail down your privacy settings and make sure people can't tag you without your approval.

DON'T BE A SLAVE TO LIKES

Social media can take you back to the teenage years – the desperate desire to be liked and to keep up with what your peers are doing. You're adulting now so rise above it. Your worth isn't

"If you are on social media, and you are not learning, not laughing, not being inspired or not networking, then you are using it wrong."

GERMANY KENT

measured by the number of likes or followers that you have. It's your friends IRL (that's 'In Real Life') that count. It's your personal successes and real-world interactions that should be what you're most proud of. Social media likes and shares are temporary self-esteem boosts (hence why we keep going back for more). You're worth so much more than that.

THANKS FOR YOUR OPINION. I'LL JUST PUT THAT IN MY "THINGS I COULDN'T CARE LESS ABOUT" FILE.

> "Everybody gets so much information all day long that they lose their common sense."
>
> GERTRUDE STEIN

YOU WENT VIRAL FOR ALL THE WRONG REASONS!

Oops. You did something unintentionally hilarious or offensive and the internet has gone crazy! (Well, your corner of it has.) Don't run and hide. Here's how to face it like a grown-up:

- If the attention is unwelcome, delete the post.

- Make an acknowledgment (if it's something funny you've done then turn it round to your benefit) or apologize as soon as you can — content on the internet travels fast.

- If it's happened at work, own up to it immediately, get advice on how best to fix it and limit any damage to your employer's reputation.

- If the barrage isn't too huge, try and respond to negative comments. Sometimes not saying anything can just make things worse.

IF IT ALL GETS TOO MUCH …

Do the adult thing and take a break. The world isn't going to collapse around you. You're not going to miss anything important. Spend some time enjoying a digital detox and get your head back in the real world.

Self-
CARE

**YOUR ADULTING GOAL
FOR THIS CHAPTER:**
*Understand the importance of self-care
for your mental, physical and emotional
wellbeing.*

WHAT IS SELF-CARE?

Self-care (not to be confused with selfishness) is so important
for your wellbeing. It means different things to different people.
For some, it's going for a 5km run and for others it's a hot bath
with a good book. It's about looking after your own happiness and
wellbeing, especially during times of stress. It's something that can
be incorporated into your everyday life, and that should hopefully
put you in a good place for managing stressful and challenging
periods when they strike. As an adult, you must take responsibility
for your own wellbeing – no one else will, it's down to you.

At the most basic level, self-care is all those simple things like
brushing your teeth, getting enough sleep, drinking enough water
or staying on top of your daily adulting responsibilities. When
we find life difficult and feel overwhelmed, it can be hard to
accomplish these things. The bigger tasks like meeting a deadline
or socializing can be even harder.

Self-care is also being patient and compassionate with yourself. It's easy to feel guilty or chastise ourselves for not meeting the standards we set, but at times like these, it's even more vital to be kind to ourselves. Take time to de-stress and indulge and you'll reap the benefits inside and out.

SIMPLE IDEAS FOR SELF-CARE

You don't need permission to look after yourself. Find what works for you and incorporate it into your life:

- Never feel guilty about taking a nap. Recharging with a 20-minute power nap can provide a significant boost. But obviously not at your desk, whilst driving, etc.

- Learn some simple yoga techniques. The Sun Salutation sequence is great for calm and relaxation, easy to remember and isn't too taxing.

- Take time to practice relaxation breathing or meditation. A simple but immensely relaxing sequence is to breathe in through your nostrils to the count of four, pause, then breathe out through your nostrils for four.

> "Rest and self-care are so important ... You cannot serve from an empty vessel."
>
> ELEANOR BROWN

■ Get into the great outdoors. Tramp through a forest, jog along a beach, hike a trail or even pace the city. Blow the cobwebs away.

WHEN MAKING NEW FRIENDS IS A BIT MORE TRICKY THAN WHEN YOU WERE AT SCHOOL.

— — —

MOM: YOU SHOULD TRY TO GET OUT A BIT MORE AND MEET SOME PEOPLE.

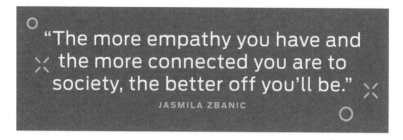

"The more empathy you have and the more connected you are to society, the better off you'll be."

JASMILA ZBANIC

CONNECT WITH OTHERS

Friends are an important support network. Connecting with them – whether it's a quiet movie night at home, a big night out or even just a text – can provide a real mood boost. If you don't have friends close by – maybe you've moved somewhere for a new job – then avoid loneliness by joining in with local events, clubs or sports teams where you can find people who share your interests.

IT'S OKAY NOT TO BE OKAY

No one can be perfectly happy all the time, that's not human. If you're trying your best to practice self-care but still find yourself feeling unhappy or anxious or that you can't cope, talk to someone. Don't leave it until you become overwhelmed. No one expects you to cope alone – it's a myth that adults should be able to keep calm and carry on. It's perfectly okay to share how you're feeling with someone you trust, perhaps a family member, close friend or your doctor. You'll be surprised what a difference it can make. The internet is also a fount of information and sources of help. Reach out in whichever way feels most comfortable for you at that moment in time. Remember that there's no need to feel embarrassed about not being able to cope or to feel you're a failure – you're certainly not alone.

Let's get
PHYSICAL

**YOUR ADULTING GOAL
FOR THIS CHAPTER:**
*Understand the simple lifestyle and health
choices that will (hopefully) prolong your
tenure as an adult.*

In the last chapter, you found out how important self-care is for
the mind. Now's the turn of your body. Just as positive mental
wellbeing helps you nail adulting, taking responsibility for your
physical wellbeing is equally vital. As much as we hate to think
about old age, the better you take care of your body now, the
fewer aches and pains you'll have when you're older. Add that
to the benefits to your mental health and what's stopping you
putting a pair of trainers on right now?!

BENEFITS OF EXERCISE – ALL YOU NEED TO KNOW

Pretty straight forward, proven and hard to argue about (so no
excuses please):

- Improves your mood and combats anxiety thanks to the
  surge of endorphins and increased sensitivity to serotonin.

- Builds muscles and strong bones, and may help prevent
  osteoporosis.

- Increases energy levels (perfect for when you're working hard at adulting).

- Can reduce the risk of chronic disease, e.g. Type 2 diabetes.

- Improves blood flow to the brain, and helps memory and mental function.

- Helps you sleep better.

- Boosts your sex drive. Miiaaoow.

CAN'T AFFORD THE GYM?

Don't throw the sweaty towel in so easily. Just put your adult thinking cap on and come up with an alternative. You can walk, jog or run for no more than the price of a pair of trainers – with all the benefits of fresh air. Get together with a friend and play tennis on a public court. Join a weekend league soccer team. Swim. Borrow a friend's dog and take it for long walks. Take the stairs rather than the elevator. There's no excuse for not getting some form of physical exercise so put away the chips, get up off your couch and start taking responsibility for your own wellbeing.

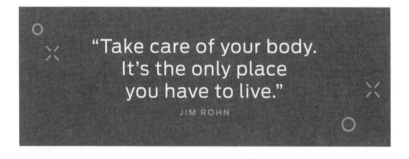

"Take care of your body.
It's the only place
you have to live."

JIM ROHN

DO MORE OF THIS ...

- Drinking lots of water.

- Devouring fruit and vegetables.

- Grilling lean meat and fish.

- Choosing wholegrain food and low-fat dairy products.

- Enjoying the good fats from foods like avocado, olive oil, fatty fish and nuts.

- Going to bed earlier and getting a good night's sleep.

DO LESS OF THIS ...

- Downing endless caffeinated drinks.

- Munching chips, sweets and chocolate on the couch.

- Spooning in the sugar.

- Bingeing on alcohol.

- Chewing on red meat.

- Burning the candle at both ends.

That said, what's great about adulting is that YOU get to make the choices. Thinking about your long-term health, you ought to be swaying towards the sensible decision to choose a healthy lifestyle. But if a whole weekend spent drinking far too much wine with good friends has the effect of lifting your mood for two solid weeks then that's self-care too, and it shouldn't be dismissed as bad for you.

DON'T PUT OFF MAKING AN APPOINTMENT

Adulting requires you to be responsible for your health, not just for your sake but for anyone else – your children or maybe elderly parents – who depends on you.

ADULTING: THAT MOMENT WHEN YOU FIND THE PERFECT AVOCADO IN THE SUPERMARKET.

If something doesn't seem right, make an appointment with your doctor. If a tooth is causing you grief, get a dentist to look at it. Don't leave it too late because 'it's nothing' and you're too lazy to pick up the phone. Be proactive about your health — no one's going to make appointments for you, so it's time to grow up.

HEALTH CHECKS YOU SHOULDN'T MISS

Women: cholesterol, blood pressure, cervical smear (PAP), mammogram (if you're over a certain age) and monthly checks of your breasts (done by you).

Men: cholesterol, blood pressure, prostate check, testicles — and, fellas, check your top half out too — breast cancer is not something just women get.

Don't forget your eyes! Not only for eyesight (a grown-up doesn't pretend they can see just so they don't have to buy glasses), an eye test can also pick up other health issues. The same applies to the dentist — put aside your childhood fears and get in that chair.

FOOD
and drink

YOUR ADULTING GOAL FOR THIS CHAPTER:
Learn the basics for progressing beyond things on toast and fries with everything.

Food and drink bring pleasure whatever your age, but in the world of adulting, your tastes are expected to be more sophisticated. No longer is it okay to dine daily on chicken nuggets or to serve up spaghetti hoops when friends come over for supper. Not that you need to wake up one morning transformed into a cordon bleu chef – it's more about having the range of food experience to fit in with any social situation you find yourself in and not end up with egg on your face.

TABLE ETIQUETTE

Know these basics and you'll be ready to dine with royalty:

- Wait until everyone has been served before you start to eat.

- When bamboozled by the choice of which knife, fork, or spoon to use, follow the outside-in rule – use utensils on the outside first and work your way inward.

- Fork in your left hand, prongs pointing downwards.

- Unless it's being passed to a specific person, always pass food to the right.

- Soup can be a messy social nightmare. Dip the spoon sideways at the edge of the bowl closest to you, then skim away from you. Sip from the side of the spoon.

- When you've finished eating, place the knife and fork parallel, with the handles in the 4 o'clock position on the right-hand rim of the plate.

BE YOUR OWN CHEF

Eating out or getting takeouts is undoubtedly fabulous and saves on cooking. The fact remains though that it's cheaper and healthier to cook for yourself. AND it gives you the skills you need to prove to others that you've mastered this adulting lark. You don't need much in your kitchen cupboard and it doesn't need to be fancy. Simple recipes every adult should know:

Spaghetti Bolognese. Stir fries (throw in anything you have to hand – within reason!). Omelets (impress your guest with a filling of their choice). Chili con carne (remember that one-pot cooking

> "There's no better feeling in the world than a warm pizza box on your lap."
>
> KEVIN JAMES

saves on washing up). Fried rice. Chicken noodles. Roast chicken. Pancakes. Curry. Pizza dough.

BE YOUR OWN SOMMELIER

That's wine expert to you and me. It can take three long years to become a master sommelier. You've got other stuff to do so what, in a very small nutshell, do you need to know about wine to give the appearance that you know what you're talking about?

- France, Italy and Spain produce some of the best and most popular wine varieties in the world so, if in doubt, play it safe and choose a wine from one of these countries.

- The 5 characteristics of wine: 1. Sweetness. 2. Acidity – the tartness of the wine. 3. Tannins – these add the bitterness. 4. Alcohol – the throat warming and brain fuzzing bit. 5. Body – light, medium or full-bodied?

- You'll be able to taste the difference between a cheap and a medium-priced bottle of wine. But research shows that the really expensive wines are only enjoyed more by wine experts. So, don't bankrupt yourself – you won't necessarily enjoy the wine more.

- In a restaurant, you'll be offered a taste before the wine is poured. Look like a pro and don't taste it – give it a swirl and smell it. If it smells vinegary, it's 'corked' – send it back and ask for another bottle.

You don't have to be a wine snob. Try lots of varieties and find the ones you really like and enjoy – that's more important than knowing your Pigato from your Négrette.

OVERDONE IT?

Let's face it, the best way to avoid a hangover is not to drink too much. If you're cracking this adulting business, you'll know that working, looking after kids and generally getting on with life is nigh on impossible with a stonking headache and a swirling belly. But there will be occasions when you overindulge. Try these 'cures' for size:

- Drink LOTS of water before you go to bed to rehydrate.
- 'Hair of the dog' doesn't help. It just masks and delays the same pain.
- Soup – the cure all of everything! Well, good for a fragile tummy anyway.
- Fruit juice helps by giving you a sugary kick and energy.
- Avoid coffee (really? yes!). It's a diuretic so will make you lose the fluids your body desperately needs.
- The three Ss: shower, sunglasses, sleep.

WHEN YOU'VE RUN OUT OF MILK:

ME: GRANOLA WITH ICE CREAM IS PRETTY GOOD.

The dating
GAME

**YOUR ADULTING GOAL
FOR THIS CHAPTER:**
*Get to grips with dating in the adult world, and
all the joys and pitfalls that come with it.*

Ah, the dating minefield. So many things to get wrong when
you're trying so hard to get things right. Forget everything you
thought you knew as a teenager. You've grown up, as have the
people you date. There's a certain new level of sophistication
required. In the 21st century, how do you play the dating game
and win?

MODERN DATING

People meet prospective dates in a very different way these
days. The time when you'd nervously approach someone in a
bar and ask if you could buy them a drink (or gradually move
towards them on the dancefloor until they noticed you) has gone.
You've probably never lived without a mobile phone so haven't
experienced not knowing whether a date is late or just isn't
coming and you have no way of contacting them. Now people
meet on online dating sites or via apps that find you a match
within a certain radius of your home.

WHAT MAKES A GREAT
ONLINE DATING PROFILE?

■ Absolutely, definitely, 100% don't lie (or include a photo that isn't you). Most people prefer honesty so don't pretend to be someone you're not – be yourself (however weird and wonderful you are!).

■ Don't waffle on. People might get bored reading it (especially if you're not as interesting as you think). You also want to leave something for people to find out about you. Oversharing is too desperate.

■ It's not all about you. Include details about what type of person you'd like to meet.

■ If you want romance, don't be afraid to say something romantic!

HOW TO PROVE TO YOUR DATE
THAT YOU WIN AT ADULTING

If you want to see each other again, make a plan. Don't just leave it with a "let's have a drink sometime".

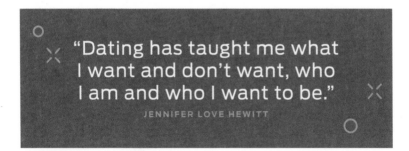

"Dating has taught me what I want and don't want, who I am and who I want to be."

JENNIFER LOVE HEWITT

Never stand them up. If you're going to be late, let them know. If you need to cancel, give them lots of notice and make an alternative plan.

Listen to them intently. Ask them questions about themselves that show you've been taking notice. Don't take calls or check your texts or play Candy Crush.

Don't forget your manners and social skills. See How Not To Be Gross, page 70.

Don't play games. If you don't want another date, make it clear – don't leave them with expectations. If you say you're going to call them, do it. Forget 'treat 'em mean, keep 'em keen' – modern dating methods mean there really are plenty more fish in the sea. Play tiresome games and you'll find your date has moved on.

WHEN IT'S NOT A MATCH

The date didn't go well. What do you do? Or, more precisely, what would an adult do? (The teenage rule book is not the one to follow anymore.)

- **Don't**: Get your mate to tell them. 'Ghost' them (the horrible practice of ending a relationship suddenly and without explanation by withdrawing from all communication).

- **Do**: Tell them in person. Be direct (without being rude). Treat them as you'd want to be treated. Don't lie, but if you do need to make up an excuse, make sure it closes down the prospect of another date completely. Use "I" so that the responsibility is on you and you're not blaming them.

In person is the best (and most grown-up way) of putting the kibosh on future dates. Use your judgement about digital methods. A text or email could be acceptable if you've only been on a couple of dates. It's definitely not respectful if you've been dating for months and your partner has already picked out the ring. You're not a child so stop hiding behind technology.

IT'S OKAY NOT TO DATE

Just because it feels like everyone else is pairing up, remember that it's okay to be happy and single. It doesn't mark you out as odd or as not having the maturity to have a relationship. In fact, self-sufficiency is a mark of winning at adulting! Nowadays, you can live your life for yourself, not with the traditional goal of an early marriage. If someone comes along who sets the tingles going, that's great, but it's not the be-all and end-all.

RELEASE
your inner child

YOUR ADULTING GOAL FOR THIS CHAPTER:

Accepting that adulting doesn't have to mean boring – there's still plenty of opportunity for silliness.

Adulting doesn't mean that you suddenly have to age 50 years. You can still enjoy all the thrills and wonder you felt as a child. In fact, reconnecting with your inner child is incredibly good for the soul and will keep you young at heart.

GREAT WAYS TO CHANNEL YOUR INNER CHILD

1. Crank up the volume and dance like your life depends on it. Sing at the top of your voice. Pretend you're Beyoncé. Whatever it takes to release those endorphins and collapse laughing.

2. Don't walk, skip! Walking can be so ... well ... pedestrian. Let the spring in your step lighten your mood. Make other people smile and spread the good vibes.

3. Laugh and laugh and laugh some more. Tell silly jokes and crack up at your own punchlines. Reminisce with friends about the stupid things you've all done, and giggle until your jaw aches and the tears run down your face.

4. Buy yourself a coloring book. Coloring is a wonderful way to calm your mind and occupy your hands. To release your inner child even more, lie on the floor to do it. Ideally with the TV on and snacks to hand.

5. Feel the exhilaration of freewheeling down a hill on a bicycle. If you ever mastered it as a child, take your hands off the handlebars. But don't close your eyes – you're not invincible, even if it does feel like it for that moment.

6. Go to a playground (with or without children in tow). Swing on a swing and feel the wind rushing past your ears. Tip back so far that the world turns upside down and the sky looks huge. Spin the roundabout as fast as you can and stay on until you stumble off with your head spinning.

7. Re-read a favorite book from your childhood. Go for the whole experience by reading it in bed, under the covers with a flashlight.

8. On a snowy day, go sledging until you're cold to the bone. Lay in the snow and make beautiful snow angels. Build a snowman. Then head inside for hot chocolate in your pajamas whilst your clothes dry out next to a blazing fire (or on the radiator if your home isn't so romantic).

9. Visit a theme park and go on all the rides you've not dared to go on since you were a child. Scream, yell, wahooo as the mood takes you. Feel the thrills and the fear, and then queue up to do it all over again.

10. We don't stop playing just because we grow up. Dig out all those games you loved playing as a child and invite friends over for a games night. Forget playing to win – just have a good belly laugh with loved ones.

Why being an adult is
AWESOME

Despite all the pressure you might feel, remember that being an adult is actually quite awesome. So, stop complaining. If you're ever in doubt or need reminding, consider these benefits of being an adult:

- Eating more than two biscuits in a row and no one stops you.

- Choosing exactly what you want to eat. Including chocolate cake for breakfast.

- Choosing what you want to wear or not wear ("yes, I am going out in this").

- Being able to choose to drink wine at 3 p.m. if the day calls for it.

- The empowerment from being able to see problems in the world and work towards solutions.

- The freedom of being able to drive a car.

- Being able to act like a child.

- Nobody telling you to tidy up your room. Or to do your homework.

- The thrill of booking vacations and choosing where to go.

- Wine!

- Winding children up.

- Knowing and learning more each and every day – and choosing which bits of that to ignore.

- Decorating your home exactly how you want.

- No bedtime curfews. And watching TV until the wee small hours.

- Wasting time in coffee shops surfing on the internet.

- Using up all the hot water when you have a shower.

- Making your own money ... and spending it on things your parents wouldn't approve of.

- Not having to ask anyone's permission to do something.

- *Being* Santa rather than believing in him.

- Explaining the world to children and seeing a sparkle in their eyes when they understand.

- Being able to appreciate your own parents more.

- You are the master of your own destiny!

> "Being an adult is mostly just going to bed when you don't want to and also waking up when you don't want to."
>
> UNKNOWN

- You can choose your friends and spring clean the toxic people out of your life.

- No more tests and exams – unless you choose to do them.

- You know what sex is, and are having it and enjoying it.

- No longer having that sinking feeling of dread that you have to tell your parents you've messed up.

- Being able to say "Because I said so" rather than having it said to you.

- Being able to phone in to something without having to "ask the permission of the adult who pays the bills".

- Being able to decide for yourself whether you are ill enough not to go to work.

- Caring less about what people think and accepting yourself.

LOOK AT ME

I'M ADULTING!